Tilly's Toolbox for Big Emotions

Dr. Ashleigh Rankin

Monk Publishing

Copyright © 2025 by Ashleigh Rankin

All rights reserved.

This workbook is intended for personal use, inclduing in educational and therapeutic settings. Photocopies of the materials may be made for individual, non-commercial purposes, such as for use in classrooms, therapy sessions, or private practice. No part of this workbook may be sold for monetary gain, reproduced, distributed, or transmitted in any form or by any means, including photocopying, recording, or other electronic or mechanical methods without prior written permission from the publisher, except as permitted by U.S. copyright law. Unauthorized copying, redistribution, or sale of this workbook, in whole or in part, is strictly prohibited. For permission requests, contact:

www.monkpublish.com

Book Cover by Ashleigh Rankin
Illustrations by Ashleigh Rankin

First Edition March 2025
ISBN: 979-8-9920683-8-2

Praise for *Tilly's Toolbox for Big Emotions*

"*Tilly's Toolbox for Big Emotions* is a fantastic resource for educators and parents looking to help children understand their emotions and develop healthy coping skills. As a retired educator with over 40 years of elementary education experience, I highly recommend this for teachers and students. Every child experiences emotions, and learning how to manage them is a crucial skill.
This resource provides valuable guidance in a clear, engaging way."
- Ollie Archambault, Master of Arts in Education

"Learning emotional self-regulation can be a challenge for children. *Tilly's Toolbox for Big Emotions* is an emotional self-regulation workbook that empowers children to navigate their emotions effectively. It uses an interactive approach with relatable stories of Tilly together with various learning activities that help children put a voice to their feelings and understand how to use positive coping skills. This book can be useful for teachers, therapists, parents, and other caregivers of children. As a developmental psychologist, I highly recommend *Tilly's Toolbox for Big Emotions* as a valuable resource for supporting children's emotional development."
- Dana Donohue, Ph.D. in Developmental Psychology

"Emotional development and coping skills are often overlooked in education, making this resource a valuable addition to any curriculum. This comprehensive, research-based workbook offers a variety of engaging activities to help children build lifelong emotional skills. Its flexibility allows teachers and parents to set the pace in both individual and group settings. A major bonus is the inclusion of extra activities and the ability to make copies, ensuring it can be easily accessed and adapted for different needs."
- Pearl Hansen, Ph.D. in Administration, Curriculum and Instruction

"This workbook is an outstanding resource for helping children develop emotional expression and regulation. As a clinical psychologist, I know how important it is for kids to understand their feelings and learn healthy coping strategies. Through interactive lessons and hands-on strategies, this workbook provides a structured, accessible way for children to build emotional awareness and resilience. I highly recommend it for parents, educators, and therapists seeking to support children's emotional growth."
- Kenneth Littlefield, PsyD

"I use this workbook regularly as a therapist. I highly recommend it for helping children build essential emotion regulation skills. With engaging activities, relatable examples, and practical strategies, it provides a supportive and fun way for kids to understand and manage their feelings.
This resource is an invaluable tool for parents, educators, and therapists looking to empower children with lifelong emotional skills."
- An Ngo, PsyD

"As a therapist, I often work with parents of children who have big feelings, which can be confusing and stressful for the whole family. This book will help parents and children learn how to navigate those emotions. Dr. Rankin has broken down complex ideas about what emotions are and how we can work with them into bite-size pieces that young learners can digest - and their parents might also learn something as well! This book can help you bond with your child and help both of you understand their feelings and how to handle them. I'm so glad this resource exists."
- Rachel Willimott, LCSW and founder of Encompass Therapy

After earning my doctorate in clinical psychology, I knew I wanted to share the knowledge I had gained to help others improve their lives. While clinical work allows one to support individuals, it is often limited by how many people it can reach. Publishing books, however, provides a way to expand that reach and make valuable information accessible to many. It is my hope that this workbook serves as a helpful resource for children who engage with it, as well as for those who aim to support children in developing their emotional skills.

As adults, we often navigate complex emotions daily, but for children, emotions can feel overwhelming and difficult to understand. Whether in the classroom, at home, or with friends, children are still learning to recognize and regulate their feelings. By teaching them how to identify, differentiate, and cope with emotions, we empower them with tools to handle their feelings in a healthier way. These skills not only foster emotional stability during childhood but also lay the foundation for a happier, healthier adulthood.

This workbook is designed to help children explore their emotions in a fun, engaging, and thoughtful way. It contains evidence-based activities and exercises, drawn from therapeutic approaches like Cognitive Behavioral Therapy (CBT) and Acceptance and Commitment Therapy (ACT), that promote emotional awareness and offer practical strategies for managing challenging emotions. The lessons and activities in this book are intended for elementary-aged children, with the understanding that skill levels can vary widely. Depending on developmental stage and emotional maturity, the amount of guidance each child needs may differ. Some may find completing activities independently easier, while others may benefit from additional support and encouragement. Upon completion of this workbook, children will build resilience, improve their emotional intelligence, and develop the confidence to face challenges with greater emotional balance.

This resource can be a valuable tool for children, and the adults who guide them on their emotional journey. Together, we can help children grow into emotionally healthy individuals, prepared to navigate the world with empathy, understanding, and confidence.

— *Dr. Ashleigh Rankin*

Important Note: You are welcome to photocopy the material in this workbook for educational or therapeutic purposes, but please do not sell or otherwise distribute the content for monetary gain. This workbook is intended for personal and professional use to support children's emotional development.
See copyright page for more information.

This workbook is designed for the content to build upon itself. It is suggested to follow the pages in order to build an understanding as one progresses through the material. The structure has been created with flexibility in mind, allowing it to be completed in various group or individual settings throughout a semester or during a series of sessions. Please note, many concepts in this workbook may be new and require time, patience, and support for children to fully grasp. Therefore, it is highly recommended to complete this workbook with the guidance of a therapist, teacher, or caregiver. Here are some tips and guidelines for using this workbook effectively:

Tips for Individual Settings

Set a Comfortable Pace: Take time to explore each concept and ensure the child fully understands before moving on to the next section. Some children may need additional time with certain activities or exercises. Allow space for questions, discussion, and reflection.

Create a Supportive Environment: Ensure the learning environment is calm and free from distractions. This helps the child stay focused and engaged.

Break It Down: If the workbook feels overwhelming, break the activities into smaller, more manageable steps. Work on one page or exercise at a time, checking in with the child regularly to ensure they feel confident.

Provide Positive Reinforcement: Offer encouragement and praise throughout the process. Acknowledge the child's efforts and progress, even if they haven't fully mastered a concept. This builds confidence and motivation to continue.

Encourage Reflection: At the end of each lesson or session, take a moment to discuss what was learned. Ask the child about their thoughts, feelings, and any challenges they faced. This helps consolidate learning and provides opportunities for growth.

Be Flexible: While the workbook is designed to be completed in a structured order, it is important to be adaptable. If a child struggles with a particular section, you may need to revisit prior concepts or take a different approach to help them understand.

Tips for Group Settings:

Foster Collaboration: In a group setting, encourage children to share their thoughts and experiences. This provides support and opportunities for peer learning.

Adapt to Different Learning Styles: Children in a group may have varying learning styles and paces. Be prepared to modify activities to meet the needs of different individuals. Provide hands-on activities, visual aids, or verbal explanations, depending on what helps the group members best.

Establish Group Norms: At the beginning of group lessons or sessions, create a safe and respectful space where everyone feels comfortable sharing. Establishing group norms, such as taking turns, listening actively, and offering constructive feedback, can promote a positive and productive environment.

Guide Group Discussions: When reviewing exercises in a group, lead discussions that encourage critical thinking and group problem-solving. Ask open-ended questions that prompt reflection, creativity, and connection to real-life experiences.

Allow for Peer Support: Encourage group members to support each other by pairing them up for certain tasks, or facilitating group work. This helps foster social skills, teamwork, and empathy.

Balance Group and Individual Time: While group activities are important, ensure that each child has time to reflect on their own understanding. Provide moments where children can work individually or in smaller pairs to focus on personal growth.

General Tips for Both Settings:

Check-In Regularly: Throughout the workbook, check in with the child or children to gauge their understanding. If they seem confused or frustrated, offer gentle redirection or guidance to ensure they don't feel stuck.

Use Creative Tools: Encourage children to express themselves through art, drawings, or other creative activities when applicable. This allows children to engage with the material in a way that resonates, deepening their connection to the concepts.

Stay Positive and Patient: Keep in mind that some concepts may take time for the child to fully understand. Be patient and supportive, offering guidance as needed without rushing through the content.

Encourage Regular Practice: To achieve best results, encourage the child or children to revisit certain sections or practices periodically. This helps reinforces new skills and concepts while allowing learning to progress.

Following these guidelines will create a positive, effective, and supportive experience for children developing their skills. The aim is to foster growth, understanding, and skill development at a pace that is comfortable and encouraging for each child.

Contents

Feelings and Emotions — 1
    Why learn about emotions.
    Physical feelings vs emotional feelings.

Primary and Secondary Emotions — 17
    What are primary and secondary emotions.
    How to identify primary and secondary emotions.

Thoughts, Actions, and Feelings — 23
    How thoughts, actions and feelings interact.
    Changing thoughts, actions, and feelings.

Coping — 31
    What is coping.
    Implementing good coping skills.

Applying Everything Together — 43
    Practicing identifying feelings, emotions, thoughts and actions, and using reframing and other coping skills.
    Bringing new skills into regular practice.

Resources and Extra Activities — 53
    Dictionary
    Additional Activities
    Extra Printable Worksheets

This book belongs to:

_____

who started working on it on this date:

_____

Tilly's Toolbox for Big Emotions

Feelings and Emotions

Learning about emotions is very important.
Emotions help us know how we
feel and how other people feel. When we
learn about emotions and how to talk
about them, it helps us make good choices.

Learn with Tilly!
She is feeling sad. She knows she is sad,
so she tells someone. Tilly gets a hug
and talks about why she is sad.
Hugging and talking makes Tilly feel better.

Learning about emotions also helps you be kind to others. When you see someone is feeling happy or sad, you can be a good friend to them. Emotions are like little clues that help us know how we feel and how others feel, too!

Tilly sees that her friend looks upset.
She asks him if something is bothering him and if he wants to talk.
After he shares why he is upset,
he starts to feel better.

Think of a time when you saw someone who was sad or upset. Maybe a friend was feeling lonely or someone got hurt. Can you draw or write about how you helped them?

What did you do?
How did it make them feel?
Maybe you said something nice to cheer them up or maybe you gave them a hug. Remember to use bright colors in your drawing, or write a few sentences about your kind actions.

How do we feel?

We can feel in many ways!

We feel things in our bodies,
like when we get hurt.
We call this physical pain.
For example, Tilly hits her elbow.
She feels a very sharp,
tingle that hurts.

We can also feel emotions
when we feel physical pain.
For example, Tilly might feel
emotional pain like feeling
angry, scared, or embarrassed
when she hit her elbow.

Tilly knows another way she can feel
physically and *emotionally*!

I can tell when I am happy!

I feel happiness *physically* in my body.
I can feel my heartbeat, and my face smile.
Sometimes, I am so happy that I cry or I feel my cheeks are hot when I am blushing!

I can also feel my emotions when I am happy!
Emotionally, I feel excited, joyful, loved, or eager!

Let's do a fun worksheet about how we feel!

We just learned 2 ways we can feel things! Can you name them?

1 _____

2 _____

Here's a Hint! The blue words on the last 2 pages!

Can you name a physical feeling you have felt in your body?

_____

_____

Can you name an emotional feeling you have felt before?

_____

_____

Answers:
2 Ways We Feel: Physical and Emotional
Physical Feelings: Sharp, Tingle, Crying, Heartbeat, Hot...
Emotional Feelings: Sad, Happy, Joyful, Eager, Love...

It's good to think about how we feel!
Let's take a moment to see how we are doing!

Today, I feel _____
_____
_____ emotionally.

_____
Physically, I feel _____
_____.

Draw or write why you feel that way.

Great job talking about your feelings! It can be hard to say how we feel. There are many words that help us share our feelings. The more we learn, the easier it is to talk about how we are feeling.

TIP! If you need to learn what a word means, look at the dictionary in the back of the book!

Let's learn new words we can use to talk about our emotions from the chart below!

Happy	Sad	Scared	Surprised	Peaceful	Angry
Cheerful	Bored	Fearful	Startled	Calm	Mad
Proud	Tired	Shy	Wowed	Loving	Grumpy
Joyful	Guilty	Nervous	Amazed	Affectionate	Upset
Eager	Disappointed	Worried	Shocked	Trusting	Annoyed
Silly	Lonely	Anxious	Confused	Relaxed	Frustrated
Content	Hurt	Regret	Overwhelmed	Caring	Irritated
Excited	Inferior	Insecure	Curious	Thoughtful	Offended
Loved	Rejected	Embarrassed	Puzzled	Valued	Jealous
Hopeful	Insignificant	Excluded	Speechless	Inspired	Hateful
Optimistic	Hopeless	Frightened	Moved	Accepted	Furious
Confident	Depressed	Panic	Awestruck	Passionate	Disgusted
Energetic	Miserable	Terrified	Stunned	Thankful	Agitated
Glad	Blue	Unsafe	Crushed	Quiet	Enraged
Upbeat	Empty	Spooked	Bewildered	Serene	Cranky

This chart teaches us new ways we can *physically* feel our emotions with our bodies!

	Happy	Smiling, jumping, dancing, energetic moving, laughing, stomach "butterflies", standing tall, fast heartbeat.
	Sad	Tears in eyes, heavy feeling in chest or body, sighing, tired, slow moving, drooping head, slumped shoulders.
	Scared	Feeling weak, shaky or trembling, goosebumps, fast breathing or heartbeat, upset stomach, lump in throat.
	Surprised	Feeling activated, energized, wide eyes or open mouth, quick breathing or heartbeat, fast movements.
	Peaceful	Relaxed muscles, slow heartbeat and breathing, happy and relaxed facial expression, calm movements.
	Angry	Hot or flushed face, clenched fists or jaw, shaking, jerky body movements, bursts of energy.

There are lots of words that describe how we feel - more than what we can see in these two charts!
Remember, when you learn more words, it helps you say how you feel.
It also helps you understand how other people feel.

Emotions Word Search

```
a h s y m x r g y l
f a a m r d p s l d
d p w x s g u e e e
n p d a m o n r n l
e y l p v r o a o d
y y k r d b a n l e
v h e x c i t e d r
f n s d u o r p f a
d e s i r p r u s c
n d i s g u s t u s
```

Find the words in the puzzle!
Words can go in any direction.
Words can share letters as they cross over each other.

Anwsers in the back of the book!

angry	excited	lonely	proud	shy
bored	fear	mad	sad	surprised
disgust	happy	nervous	scared	

Physical Feelings Word Search

k	s	d	k	y	e	c	j	e	s
q	c	h	a	c	i	o	w	l	u
b	s	i	a	e	a	l	e	i	r
i	z	g	s	k	h	d	a	m	v
s	l	e	e	p	y	t	k	s	h
y	t	s	r	i	h	t	o	u	d
l	f	t	r	e	k	d	n	h	q
j	v	a	a	r	a	g	v	j	d
n	e	r	t	i	r	e	d	h	v
t	t	q	l	y	y	m	m	u	t

Find the words in the puzzle!
Words can go in any direction.
Words can share letters as they cross over each other.

Anwsers in the back of the book!

cold   hot   sick   tear   tummy
head   hungry   sleepy   thirsty   weak
heart   shaky   smile   tired

BIG Emotions Word Search

```
s w l i e r h a y d l v r d n g o s f x
u c z o p z a d w t e i m u f o x f v e
o a s y t d p i d a l g e r a t p y w a
i l h u n t p s g e t i i l u f r a e f
r m y o c g y e c h s g u d u p s e t q
u x e e v h r q a a h i e g d e k t y d
c v f g l x e n c t r y r t i d p p r p
q x m u y p k e e d o e r p e w o w e d
t e s v z f m n r n g m d n r d v x h s
b p z p u a e f n f m h n a a u d y h y
h a e l w d q a p u u u s s w e s r n o
c w d a l s y j g l t l n g n i r a c h
d l a d c u y i l s r y k c f v o u o s
e h m e n e r j n i o r x b d v q n y x
f f l v d p f h e m s m i e z y r i h c
n s i g u k n u v a d t x n o r r z c c
z e u i t a e m l g l j h x d r r g h c
q f k j r a h i m n o o s d f d p j n p
k z j c u q o n u o z a u w w f e b l a
s p x w h r e j e c t e d s b r o h o m
```

Find the words in the puzzle!
Words can go in any direction.
Words can share letters as they cross over each other.

Anwsers in the back of the book!

angry	peaceful	fearful	curious	sad
caring	wowed	jealous	stunned	eager
glad	annoyed	thankful	mad	surprised
hurt	cheerful	shy	upset	rejected
scared	guilty	calm	frightened	happy

BIG Physical Feelings Word Search

```
j e r k y p m g y j j s k g p a y f g s
g z v w t o e t o h r x i n o k y t l h
r n x g o c l n g a t g j i a t v o a o
g n i p m u j e e v a o k h g b w a r q
h a x c j x s t e g e r s g j c u c u l
d e c v n b x r e c b w a u v v c v w q
c e f t f a s f g v t e c a h f b o y n
i n h m i m d r o v r h q l k a e w t k
x d v s i v l c b c a d b v d v f j i s
t p t l u f a r f s e e y h e a v y r l
o d i s x l e t p a h h r y f o u t e u
r n r h a a f m e t l c e g v c n s d m
g m c o t f u y r d u n l i b h v g o p
s f i h o b j e n j d e a f g h c o g e
g i i l e p m m h y t l x u w j y a o d
i n g s q b i d r k w c e t y r t t z u
g r o h l a v n f f d r d e m k z o d k
d o l i i c z y g x u o z y o o a l w l
g o n n t n e n e r g i z e d n t n u b
t g j n b d g j t x o h a j z q t t c j
```

Find the words in the puzzle!
Words can go in any direction.
Words can share letters as they cross over each other.

Anwsers in the back of the book!

activated	slow	flushed	shaky	sighing
fast	breathing	heavy	clenched	relaxed
dancing	tears	jumping	smiling	trembling
heartbeat	weak	slumped	energized	laughing
jerky	drooping	tired	goosebumps	hot

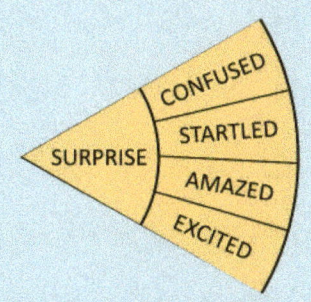
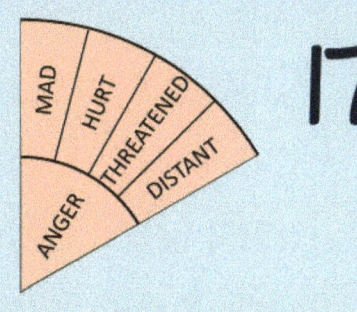

Primary Emotions and Secondary Emotions

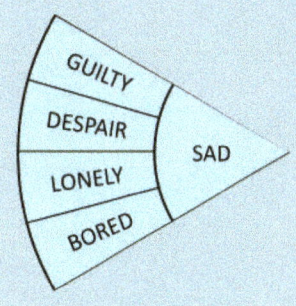
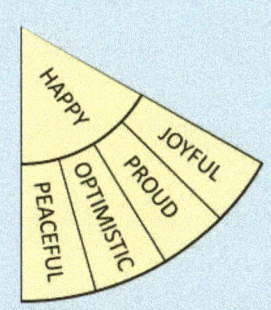
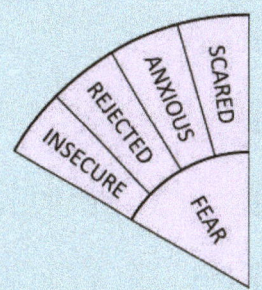
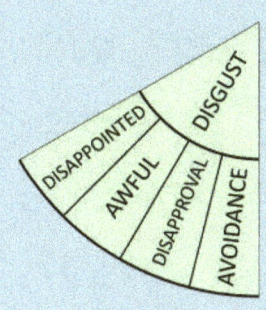

Knowing different words to describe our feelings helps us understand what we feel. Learning about *how our emotions work* can also help us understand them more clearly. Especially if we feel bad, knowing about how feelings work can help us feel better!

So, how do we learn more about how our emotions work?

A good way to understand our emotions is to think about whether we are feeling a main emotion or a feeling that comes after the main one.
We call these Primary Emotions and Secondary Emotions.

The 2 types of Emotions

Primary Emotions

How we first feel about something.

- The body's first reaction to an event or situation.
- They alert you, telling you what you need.
- You can feel them very strongly.
- Usually, these feelings do not last very long.

Example: Feeling sad when someone lies to you.

Secondary Emotions

Our second reaction to how we feel.

- Reaction to the primary emotions felt.
- Involves emotions that might be hard to notice or understand.
- These feelings can last longer than the primary emotions.

Example: Feeling frustrated about feeling sad.

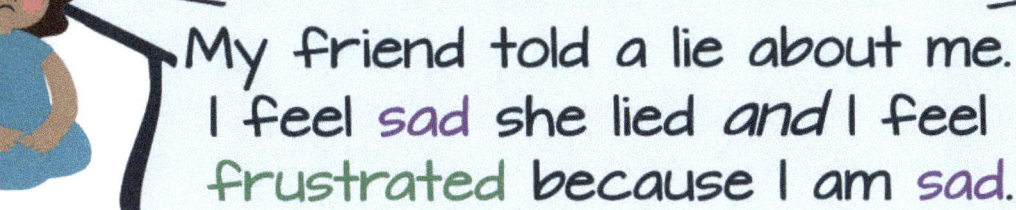

My friend told a lie about me. I feel sad she lied and I feel frustrated because I am sad.

A different way to think about
Primary Emotions and Secondary Emotions
is to look at them like colors!
There are main colors like red, blue, and yellow.
When you mix these colors together, you can make new colors. For example, red and blue make purple. Even the colors we make can be different. For instance, there can be light blue and dark blue.

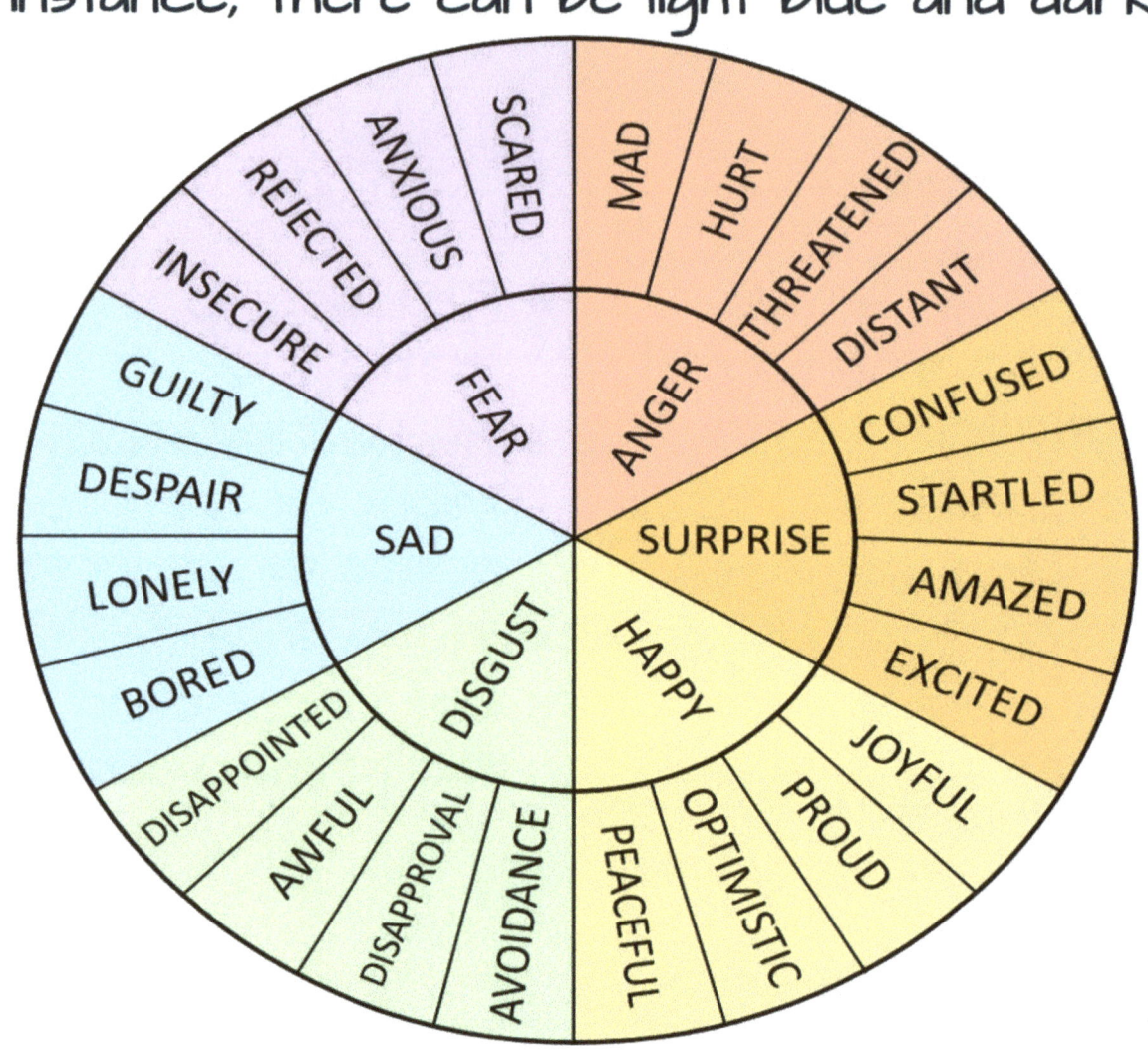

Emotions are the same!
There are Primary Emotions, and when we mix them, we can feel different things, or Secondary Emotions. For example, if we mix being happy and surprised, we might feel delight. Emotions can also feel strong or weak. For instance, feeling very happy can be called excited, while feeling a little happy can be called content.

We can see in the color wheel that there are 6 common Primary Emotions: fear, anger, surprise, happy, disgust, and sad.

There are so many Secondary Emotions that it is hard to name them all!

Here's a simple way to understand:
A Primary Emotion is the first feeling you have. It is the main feeling you feel.
A Secondary Emotion is the second feeling you have - after the first.

So, remember: the first feeling you feel is the Primary Emotion, and the second feeling is the Secondary Emotion!

Let's try to identify some Primary and Secondary Emotions!

Tilly sees her puppy running in the street.
Tilly is fearful the puppy might get hurt.
Tilly yells because she feels anxious. It scares the puppy.

Tilly's Primary Emotion is _____
(Fear)

Her Secondary Emotion is _____
(Anxious)

If Tilly knew how she felt, she could have stayed calm and talked to her puppy without scaring it!

23

Thoughts Actions and Feelings

How could Tilly have acted differently with her puppy?

First, Tilly needs to stop and think about how she feels. You and Tilly have learned how to do this by learning about Physical and Emotional feelings, and Primary and Secondary Emotions! Next, Tilly should learn how thoughts and feelings can change how we behave!

What we think and what we feel impacts how we react!

Imagine you are feeling really nervous about a test at school. You *think*, "I am going to fail!" That makes you *feel* worried! You know you are worried because you physically feel you have an upset stomach, and you emotionally feel fearful and anxious. You decided to *react* by not studying or trying your best.

Now, let's try to change that thought and see how we feel and act. Instead of _thinking_, "I am going to fail," you can think, "I can try my best and do okay." When you think that, you _feel_ a little better and maybe even feel brave enough to give it a try! You decide to _react_ by studying hard and trying your best.

Can you think of a time when you felt upset because of something you were thinking, and it made you act in a way you did not like?

Draw or write about it in the box above.

The way we think and feel can change how we act! The way we act can also change how we think and feel!

Imagine Tilly has to take a test at school. During the test, Tilly _acts_ like she does not care about her grade. She throws her pencil, or guesses instead of trying her best. After the test, Tilly notices she _feels_ sad and guilty because she did not try hard. She _thinks,_ "I am a bad person!" That makes her _feel_ worse!

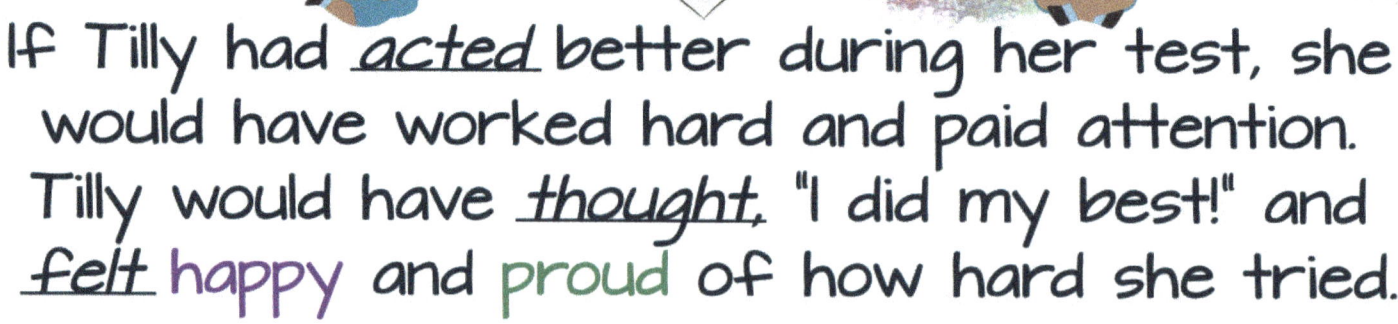

If Tilly had _acted_ better during her test, she would have worked hard and paid attention. Tilly would have _thought,_ "I did my best!" and _felt_ happy and proud of how hard she tried.

Our thoughts, feelings, and actions work in a circle. What this means is:

Our thoughts, feelings, and actions all work together to help decide how we feel and act!

Why is it important to learn this? If we can understand how we think, feel, and act, and see how they are connected, we can learn to change our thoughts to help us feel and act better!

Let's practice changing our thoughts with Tilly!

What happened?
My friend, Joy, has not spoken with me much this week.

Tilly thought, "Joy has not talked with me much this week. She must be mad at me."

Tilly felt, sad and lonely, and angry and hurt.

Because Tilly was upset, she ignored Joy and avoided her at school.

Just because Tilly has this thought does not mean it is true. If Tilly can come up with new thoughts, she can see the situation differently.

	New Thoughts	New Feelings	New Actions
#1	"Joy might be upset with me, but maybe she is not. I do not know."	Fearful or worried Joy might be upset with me, but not as angry or hurt.	Ask Joy if she is upset with me, or if there is another problem.
#2	"Joy has probably been busy with school or soemthing else."	Sad or lonely because Joy and I have not talked, but I understand.	Joy and I will stay friends, and I will be nice and still say "hi" when I see her.
#3	"Maybe Joy is upset about something unrelated to me."	Fearful or worried for Joy and how she may be feeling.	Ask Joy if she would like to talk about it, or if I can help.

Now, you try changing your thoughts, just like Tilly!

What happened?

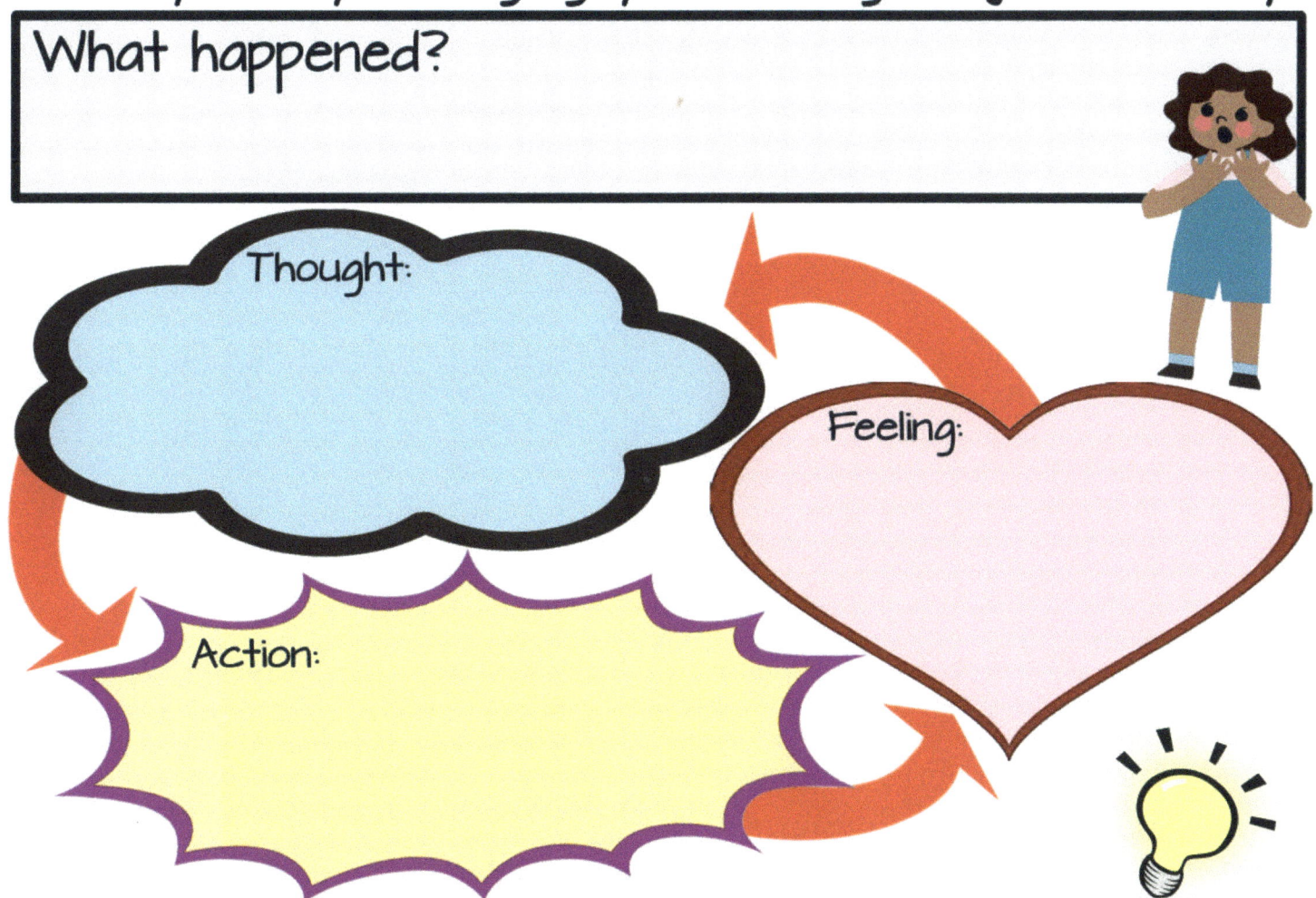

Remember, just because you think it does not mean it is true.
Try to come up with new thoughts to see what might change.

	New Thoughts	New Feelings	New Actions
#1			
#2			
#3			

Coping

Let's Review!

So far, we have learned:

-> How to tell what we are feeling by naming our Physical and Emotional feelings.

-> How to sort Primary Emotions and Secondary Emotions.

-> How our thoughts, feelings, and actions work together.

-> How to change our thoughts, feelings, and actions to help us understand something or feel better.

Great Job! You have worked really hard!

All of these skills are really helpful to learn! They help us to understand and cope with our emotional and physical feelings. The more we practice understanding our own emotions, the better we become at expressing and coping with our emotions!

What is Coping? How do we cope?

Coping is your way of learning to work with your feelings so you can feel better!

Here are some ways we can cope:
-> <u>Talking to someone</u> we trust, like a friend.
-> <u>Taking deep breaths</u> to calm down.
-> <u>Doing something fun</u> like drawing.
-> <u>Taking a break</u> when things feel too much.

 Different emotions use different types of coping.

The great thing about coping is you can pick what you like! There are many ways to do it, you just have to find those that work best for you!

Let's explore!

We will find your favorite ways to cope!

We will start by learning about different ways we can cope!

Active Coping Ideas

- Walking
- Running
- Hiking
- Yoga
- Stretching
- Jumping
- Dancing
- Jump Rope
- Squeezing a Stress Ball
- Hula Hoop
- Playing a Sport
- Tag
- Playing with a Ball
- Riding a Bike

Active Coping is anything that gets you moving and helps you feel better!

Can you think of other Active Coping ideas to write in the box below?

Social Coping Ideas

Social Coping is any activity you can do with someone else that helps you feel better!

- Read a Book with Someone
- Watch a Movie with Siblings
- Call your Best Friend
- Eat Dinner with Family
- Cook or Bake with a Friend
- Play a Game with Family
- Cuddle or Play with your Pet
- Have a Sleepover
- Video-Chat with Family
- Share your Feelings with Someone you Trust

Relaxing Coping Ideas

Deep Breathing -> This is taking big, deep breaths. Close your eyes and count each breath to 10. Start over as needed. To practice, try <u>flower/candle</u> in the back of the book!

Guided Imagery -> This is using your imagination to think about a calm, happy place.
You can rest quietly, or even nap while you think about a happy place.
If you need help thinking of one, you can listen to a story, read, or look at pictures of places you like.

Relax your Muscles -> Relaxing our muscles helps us feel better! We can do this many ways! Squeeze your muscles real tight and count to 5. After 5, stop squeezing them and feel them relax. Taking a bath is also relaxing!

Other Ways to Relax -> Listening to Music
Blowing Bubbles
Drinking Cold Water
Counting Backwards
Watching a Funny Movie
Meditating (Sitting quietly as long as you can.)

Draw or write about your favorite way to relax!

Creative Coping Ideas

Color, Draw, or Paint
Write a Poem, Play, Story, or Song
Play an Instrument
Create with Clay, Sand, or Play-Doh
Engage Your Senses
 -> _Touch_ different textures (like rice or shaving cream), or splash cold water on your face. Count everything you can _see_ in a certain color (like everything blue you see). _Listen_ and try to guess the sounds you hear. _Taste_ your favorite food or drink. _Smell_ something good, like a flower or your clean blanket!
Invent Something -> A New Game, Toy, Anything!
Journal -> Write about Your Thoughts, Feelings, or What Happened During Your Day.

Let's try journaling together!

Today's date is: _____

The weather today was _____

One thing I did today was _____
_____

It made me feel _____

Tomorrow, I would like to _____
_____

Ideas for Coping with Negative Thoughts

Let's talk about dealing with bad thoughts. Sometimes, we all have bad thoughts, and that is okay! If you try to pretend they are not there, they might get bigger. If you talk about them and think of something good instead, those bad thoughts will not bother you as much.

Thinking happy thoughts helps the bad ones go away!

Reframing -> This is when you think about the good instead of the bad. An example: instead of thinking, "I am stuck at home," try thinking something good like, "I am lucky I am home with my toys!"

Acceptance -> This means you pay attention to the things you can change, and accept the things you cannot change. An example: imagine you really want to play at the park but it is raining. You cannot stop the rain, but you can accept that it is raining. Instead of feeling upset, you can find something fun to do inside, like drawing or playing a game!

Self-Care -> This is how we take good care of ourselves. It is something that we need to do every day! Things like playing outside, eating healthy foods, taking a bath, reading a book, or playing with a friend are good ways to care for yourself!

Other Ways to Cope with Negative Thoughts:
- -> Think about something that makes you happy. Maybe this is something that happened, something you are excited about, or someone you love.
- -> Practice Gratitude: this means being thankful for good things in your life. You can write them down, draw them, or just think about the great people and things you have.
- -> Read, watch, or listen to something that is funny. Tell jokes with your family or friends. Laughing helps us feel better!

There are lots of ways to feel better, even more than what are in this book! Now that we know some ways to cope, let's learn how to use them! Different feelings and situations use different ways to cope. It is good to try a few and see which ones help you the most!

Let's learn with Tilly!

Tilly is really mad! She feels angry and hurt. Help Tilly by circling the best way to cope! Tilly can cope by:

Throwing Something   Talking to Someone   Reading

Throwing something will not help Tilly deal with what is upsetting her. Reading a book will distract her, but it will not help fix why she is upset. Talking with someone about feeling angry and hurt will help Tilly feel better!

Tilly is feeling worried. She is fearful and scared. Tilly can cope by:

Writing in her Journal   Running Away   Dancing

Running away is just avoiding and will not help Tilly deal with feeling worried. Dancing might distract her, but it will not help her fix what is worrying her. Journaling about what she fears and why she is scared will help Tilly fix it!

Tilly is crying. She feels sad and lonely. Tilly can cope by:

Coloring   Yelling and Acting Out   Taking Deep Breaths

Coloring might distract Tilly, but it will not help her fix why she is sad. Yelling and acting out is not helpful and Tilly will not feel better. Taking deep breaths will help Tilly stop crying so she can fix feeling sad.

Finding ways to cope is like learning any other skill... it takes practice!

Sometimes, you will try a coping skill that does not work for you. That is okay! You can just try another!

List 5 of your favorite coping skills in the blue boxes below:	List 5 coping skills you want to try in the yellow boxes below:

Let's help Tilly!

Draw a line to match what happened with the best *coping* skill for Tilly to use!

What happened:

- Tilly lost her favorite toy.
- Tilly feels nervous before a big test.
- Tilly is feeling really angry.
- Tilly does not want to do her homework.
- Tilly had a bad dream and feels scared.
- Tilly has a lot to do and feels like it is too much.

Coping Skills:

- Take a few deep breaths.
- Talk to a grown-up about how she feels.
- Close her eyes and imagine a happy place.
- Take a break and do something fun.
- Ask for help from a friend or teacher.
- Count to 10 and try to calm down.

Good job helping Tilly!

Remember, everyone uses different ways to feel better! What helps Tilly when she is upset might be different from what helps her friend. It is the same with you and your friends! What helps you might be different from what your friend, brother, sister, or your Mom or Dad like to do to feel better. There is no wrong anwser when picking how to cope! If it helps and is safe, then it is a good coping skill!

Look at each sentence below. Then, circle the coping skill that will help YOU.

1. You feel sad because you lost your favorite toy. What can you do to feel better?

   Take deep breaths   Draw a picture   Take a nap

2. You are feeling nervous about going to a new place. What will help you feel calm?

   Talk to a grown-up   Hug your pet   Play with a toy

3. You are mad because someone took your crayons. What will help you calm down?

   Count to 10   Play a video game   Eat a snack

4. You do not want to do homework. You feel annoyed. What can help you feel better?

   Take a break   Ask for help   Talk to a friend

Bonus: What is one more thing you like to do to feel better? _____

Applying Everything Together

Wow! You have learned so much!

Now, you can:

1. Tell apart your physical feelings and emotional feelings.

2. You can sort your emotional feelings into two types: Primary Emotions and Secondary Emotions.

3. You know how your thoughts, feelings, and actions work together. You also know how to change your thoughts to help you feel better!

4. You can pick coping skills and use them when different things happen to help you feel better!

No matter what happens, you can always feel better!

Let's use everything you have learned!

Instructions:
1. Think about how you feel.
2. Write down or circle your feelings.
3. Use your coping skills to help you feel better.

How do you feel right now?

Physical Feelings:
- Relaxed
- Sweaty
- Weak
- Fast Heartbeat
- Slow Heartbeat
- Head Hurts
- Upset Stomach
- Sleepy
- Cold
- Hot

Other: _____

Emotional Feelings:
- Angry
- Excited
- Disgusted
- Happy
- Surprised
- Fearful
- Frustrated
- Loved
- Calm
- Sad

Other: _____

Circle your **primary emotions** (what you feel first):

Happy   Surprise   Sad   Disgust   Fear   Anger   Other:_____

Circle your **secondary emotions** (what comes after):

Joyful   Proud   Peaceful   Excited   Amazed   Confused
Startled   Mad   Hurt   Threated   Distant   Scared   Guilty
Anxious   Rejected   Lonely   Bored   Avoidant   Other:_____

What emotion do you want to feel? _____

What **coping** skill can you use to feel better?
_____
_____

Think about a time you felt angry or sad.

Draw how you felt on the person.
Draw what your face looked like.
Draw arrows pointing to the physical feelings you felt in your body.

What primary emotion did you feel?
_____
_____

Which secondary emotions did you feel?
_____
_____

What thought did you have?
_____
_____

How did you react or behave? What did you do?
_____
_____

Let's try coping by reframing our thoughts. Remember, this means to try and think a good thought instead of a bad one. How can you change your thought to help you feel better? What can you think that is good?
_____
_____

How do you feel after reframing your thought?
_____
_____

Can you write about another coping skill you could have used?
_____
_____

Sometimes, we react in ways we regret or wish we did not. One time, Tilly did this! She was mad at a friend and threw a toy car. Let's pretend Tilly has a time machine! We are going to go back in time with Tilly and change what happened!

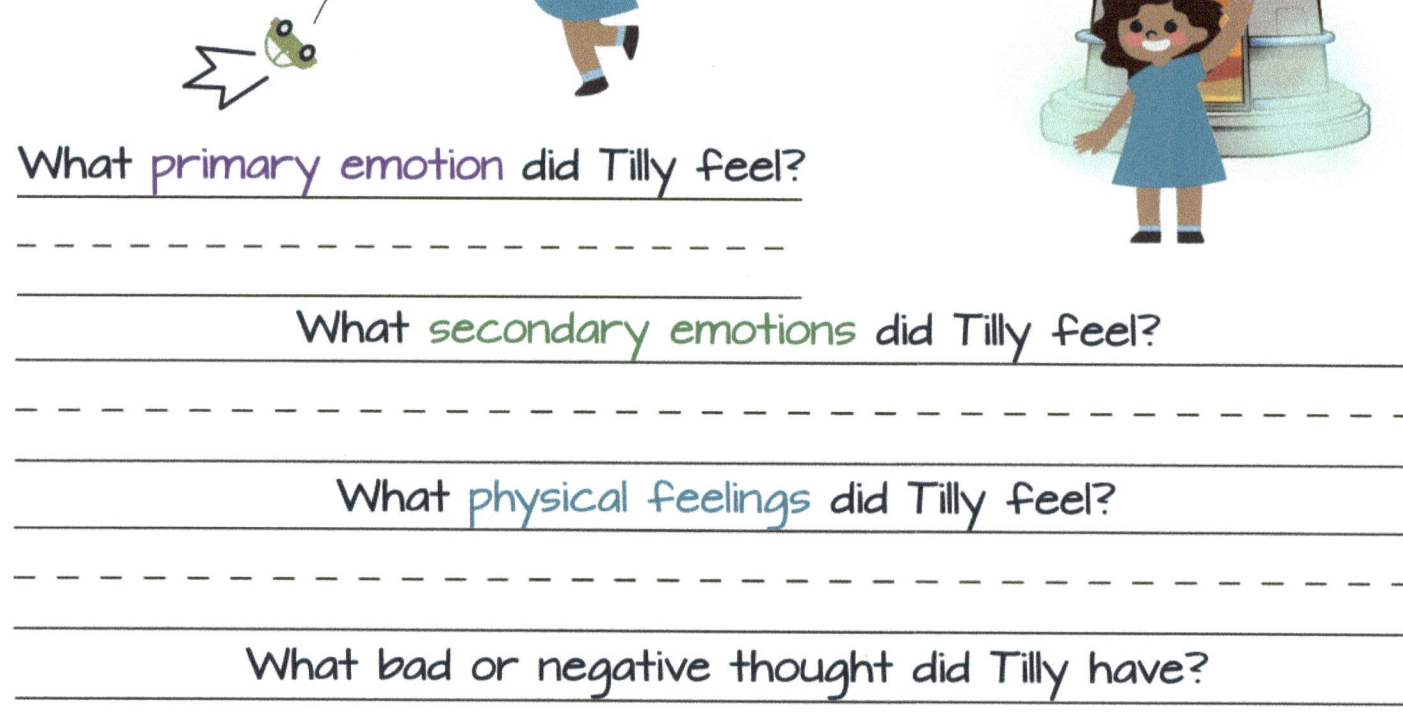

What primary emotion did Tilly feel?

What secondary emotions did Tilly feel?

What physical feelings did Tilly feel?

What bad or negative thought did Tilly have?

After using the time machine, what good thought does Tilly have?

How does this make Tilly feel now?
What primary and secondary emotions does she feel?

Instead of throwing the toy, how does Tilly act or behave after reframing her thoughts to good ones?

Name one other way Tilly can cope and not throw a toy.

It is normal to sometimes react in ways we regret or do things we wish we did not do. We should learn from them so we can try not to react or behave that way in the future!
Can you think of a time you reacted to something that happened and later you felt bad for how you acted or behaved?
Let's pretend now YOU have a time machine!
We are going back in time to change your reaction!
What happened?

_____

_____

What *primary emotion* did you feel?

_____

What *secondary emotions* did you feel?

_____

What *physical feelings* did you feel?

_____

What bad or negative thought did you have?

_____

After using the time machine, what good thought do you have?

_____

How does this make you feel now?
What *primary* and *secondary* emotions do you feel?

_____

Instead of reacting in a way that made you feel bad, how do you act or behave after *reframing* your thoughts?

_____

Name one other way you *cope* if this happens again.

_____

Emotion Regulation Wiz Kid Award

_____

has successfully completed
Tilly's Toolbox for Big Emotions
and has demonstrated
great effort and growth in
understanding and managing emotions.

Congratulations on your hard work and dedication!

Presented on this day,_____

By,_____

Resources and Extra Activities

**Photocopies of the materials may be made
for individual, non-commercial purposes, such as for use
at home, in classrooms, therapy sessions, or private practice.**
No part of this workbook may be sold for monetary gain,
reproduced, distributed, or transmitted in any form
or by any means. See copyright page for more information.

DICTIONARY
Words that start with the letters "A" through "E":

Accepted: Feeling you belong with others, like when people are nice to you.
Activated: Feeling full of energy and ready to move, like when you play tag.
Afraid: Feeling scared, like when you hear something spooky.
Agitated: Feeling upset and fidgety, like waiting too long for a turn.
Amazed: Feeling so surprised and happy because something is really great.
Angry: Feeling mad or upset, like when something is not fair.
Annoyed: Feeling bothered or irritated, like when someone keeps poking you.
Anxious: Feeling really worried or nervous, like before going to the doctor.
Awestruck: Feeling amazed and in wonder, like when you see a rainbow.
Blue: Feeling sad, like when you miss someone or something.
Bored: Not having anything fun to do, like when you finish all your games.
Calm: Feeling relaxed and peaceful, like when you sit quietly by yourself.
Caring: Being kind and thinking about others, like when you help a friend.
Cheerful: Smiling and being friendly, like when you are in a good mood.
Clenched: Holding something tight, like your fists when you are angry.
Confident: Believing in yourself, like when you know you can do something.
Confused: Feeling like you do not understand, like you cannot solve a puzzle.
Content: Feeling okay and not needing anything else, like after a nice snack.
Cranky: Feeling irritable, like when you are tired or grumpy.
Crushed: Feeling very sad and hurt, like when something you love is gone.
Curious: Wanting to know more, like when you want to learn something new.
Depressed: Feeling very sad for a long time and nothing is fun anymore.
Disappointed: Feeling let down, like when it rains on a picnic or plans change.
Disgusted: Feeling grossed out, like when something smells bad.
Drooping: Slouching or feeling low, like when you are tired.
Energized: Feeling full of power and ready to go, like before a big game.
Excited: Feeling full of energy and happiness, like before a trip or party.
Excluded: Feeling left out, like when you are not invited to play with others.

DICTIONARY
Words that start with the letters "F" through "Pa":

<u>Fearful</u>: Feeling scared, like when you hear a loud noise in the dark.

<u>Frightened</u>: Feeling very scared, like when you think about a scary story.

<u>Frustrated</u>: Feeling upset because something is hard or not working.

<u>Glad</u>: Happy and pleased, like when you see your friend.

<u>Goosebumps</u>: Tiny bumps that appear on your skin, like when you are cold.

<u>Grumpy</u>: Feeling grouchy or annoyed, like when you are really tired.

<u>Guilty</u>: Feeling bad because of something you did, like when you tell a lie.

<u>Hateful</u>: Feeling like you really do not like something or someone.

<u>Head</u>: The top part of your body where your brain and face are.

<u>Hopeless</u>: Feeling like things will never get better, like when something does not work no matter how hard you try.

<u>Hurt</u>: Feeling bad or in pain, like when you fall and scrape your knee.

<u>Inferior</u>: Feeling like you are not as good as others, like when you cannot do something as well as a friend.

<u>Insecure</u>: Feeling unsure of yourself, like thinking you are not good enough.

<u>Inspired</u>: Feeling excited to do things, like when you see something amazing.

<u>Jealous</u>: Feeling bad because you want what someone else has, like when they get a bigger piece of cake.

<u>Jerky</u>: Moving in sudden, sharp ways, like when you are nervous.

<u>Laughing</u>: Making noise because something is funny, like hearing a joke.

<u>Lonely</u>: Feeling like no one is there, like when you play by yourself.

<u>Loving</u>: Feeling caring, like when you hug someone you care about.

<u>Mad</u>: Feeling upset or angry, like when someone takes your toy.

<u>Miserable</u>: Feeling really bad, like when everything goes wrong in one day.

<u>Moved</u>: Feeling touched or emotional, like when you hear a sad story.

<u>Nervous</u>: Feeling a little scared or worried, like before a big test.

<u>Optimistic</u>: Thinking things will get better, even when things are hard.

<u>Panic</u>: Feeling out of control or scared, like when you lose something.

<u>Passionate</u>: Feeling full of energy about something, like your favorite movie.

DICTIONARY
Words that start with the letters "Pe" through "W":

<u>Peaceful</u>: Feeling calm and relaxed, like when you sit in a quiet room.
<u>Proud</u>: Feeling good about something you did, like when you get good grades.
<u>Puzzled</u>: Feeling confused or unsure, like when you cannot figure out why.
<u>Regret</u>: Feeling bad you did or did not do something, like breaking a promise.
<u>Rejected</u>: Feeling like no one wants you, like when no one picks you to play.
<u>Relaxed</u>: Feeling calm and peaceful, like when you are lying on a soft pillow.
<u>Sad</u>: Feeling like you might cry, like when your pet is sick or you lose a toy.
<u>Scared</u>: Feeling afraid, like when you hear something spooky.
<u>Shame</u>: Feeling bad after doing something wrong, like hiding a toy you broke.
<u>Shocked</u>: Feeling surprised in a way you cannot believe, like a suprise party.
<u>Shy</u>: Feeling nervous when talking to new people or being in front of others.
<u>Sighing</u>: Taking a big breath, like when you are tired, sad, or frustrated.
<u>Smiling</u>: Moving your mouth up into a happy face, like when you feel good.
<u>Surprised</u>: Feeling shocked or amazed, like when you open a present.
<u>Terrified</u>: Feeling very, very scared, like when you see a scary movie.
<u>Thoughtful</u>: Doing something nice for someone, like giving them a present.
<u>Tired</u>: Feeling sleepy and needing rest, like after a long day of playing.
<u>Trusting</u>: Being sure of someone, like your parents taking care of you.
<u>Upbeat</u>: Feeling happy and positive, like when you are having a good day.
<u>Valued</u>: Feeling special to someone, like how you feel about your best friend.
<u>Weak</u>: Feeling like you do not have energy, like when you are really sick.
<u>Worried</u>: Feeling like something can go wrong, like you might get in trouble.
<u>Wowed</u>: Feeling amazed or impressed, like when a friend does a trick.

DICTIONARY
Sayings or Phrases:

<u>Bursts of energy</u>: Quick moments of lots of energy, like jumping jacks.

<u>Fast breathing</u>: Breathing quickly, like after running a race.

<u>Slow breathing</u>: Breathing slowly, like holding your breath.

<u>Facial expression</u>: How your face looks when you feel something, like smiling when you are happy or frowning when you are sad.

<u>Fast heartbeat</u>: Your heartbeat speeds up, like when you run really fast.

<u>Slow heartbeat</u>: Your heartbeat slows down, like when you are sleeping.

<u>Hot or flushed</u>: Feeling warm or red, like when you blush because you are excited or embarrassed.

<u>Lump in throat</u>: A feeling like something is stuck in your throat when there is nothing there, like when you are about to cry.

<u>Relaxed muscles</u>: Feeling your body is loose and not stiff, like when you rest or take a nap.

<u>Shaky or trembling</u>: Feeling like your body is shaking, like when you are really cold, really scared, or really excited.

<u>Slow-moving</u>: Moving slowly because you do not have much energy, like after running or playing for a long time.

<u>Slumped shoulders</u>: Shoulders bent down, like when you are feeling sad.

<u>Standing tall</u>: Standing up straight and looking proud, like when you present at school or perform for your parents.

<u>Stomach "butterflies"</u>: A funny, fuzzy feeling in your stomach, like when you talk in front of others or go on a scary ride.

<u>Tears/tearful</u>: Crying, like when you feel sad or hurt.

<u>Tense muscles</u>: Feeling your body is tight and stiff, like when you squeeze your arm muscle to show off how strong you are.

<u>Upset stomach</u>: Feeling sick in your stomach, like when you are worried, sick, or eat spoiled food.

Emotions Word Search Anwsers

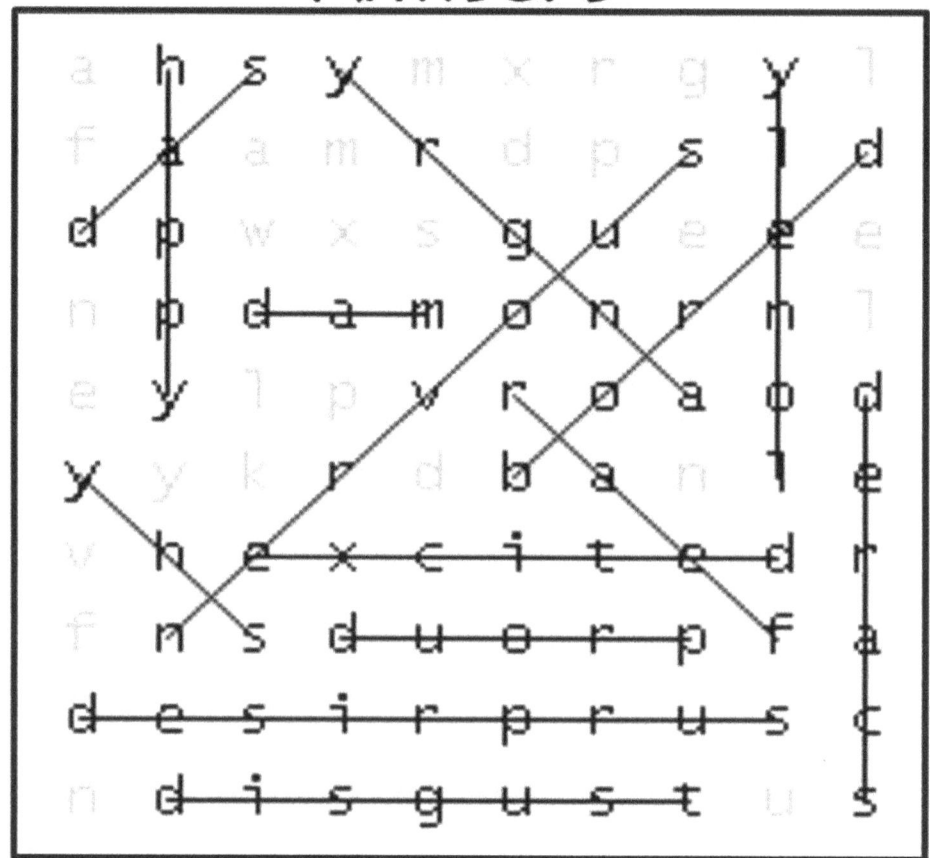

Physical Feelings Word Search Anwsers

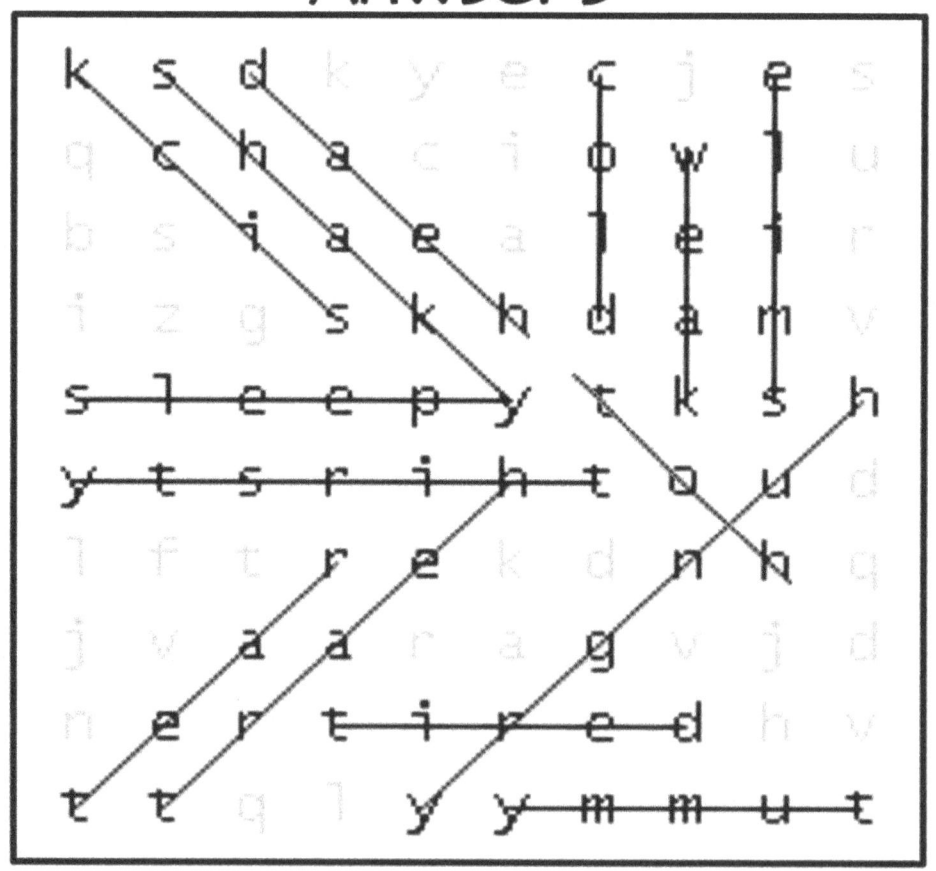

BIG Emotions Word Search Anwsers

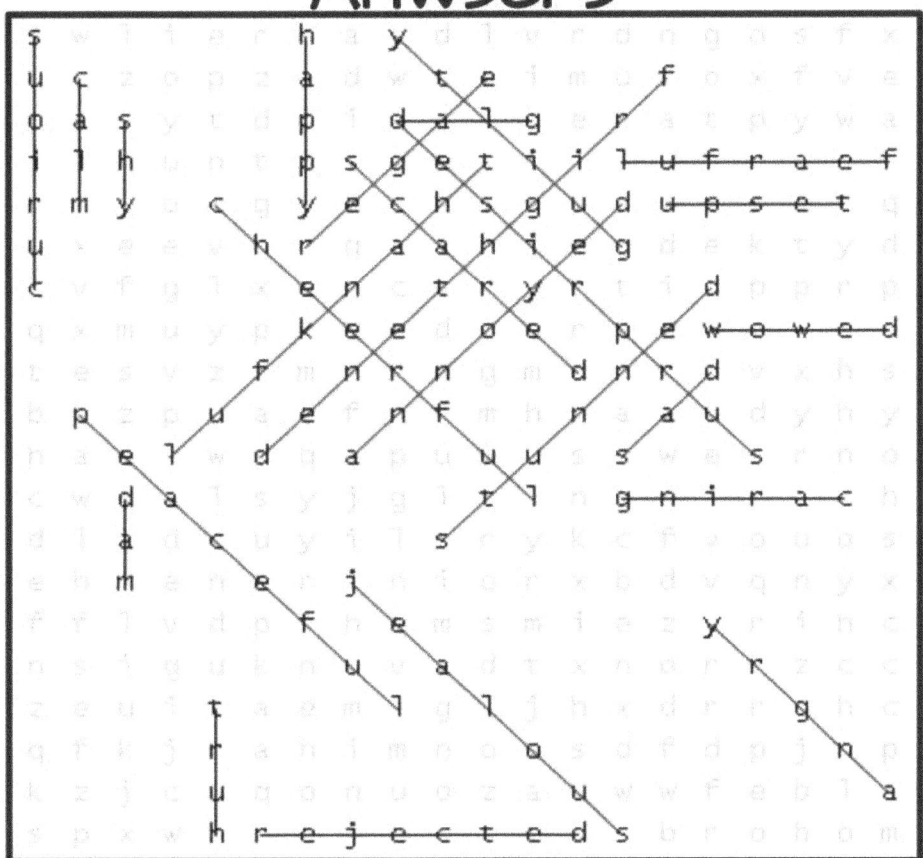

BIG Physical Feelings Word Search Anwsers

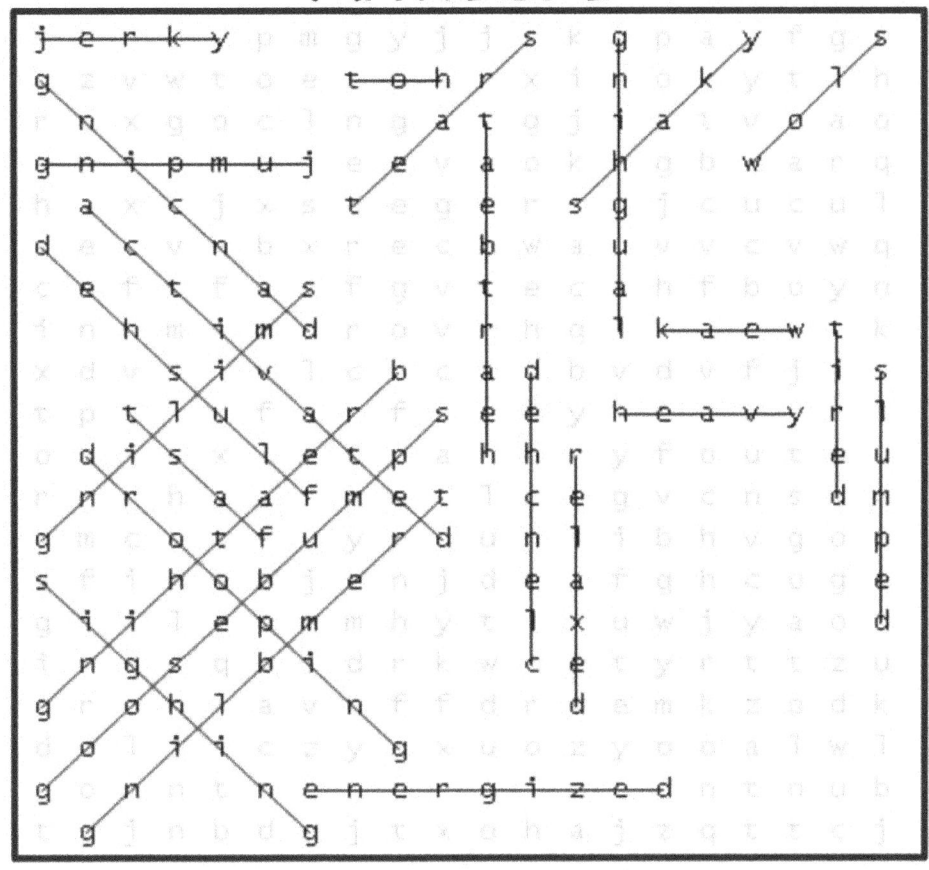

Primary Emotions and Secondary Emotions Color Wheel

Fill in the blank boxes with other Secondary Emotions you use!

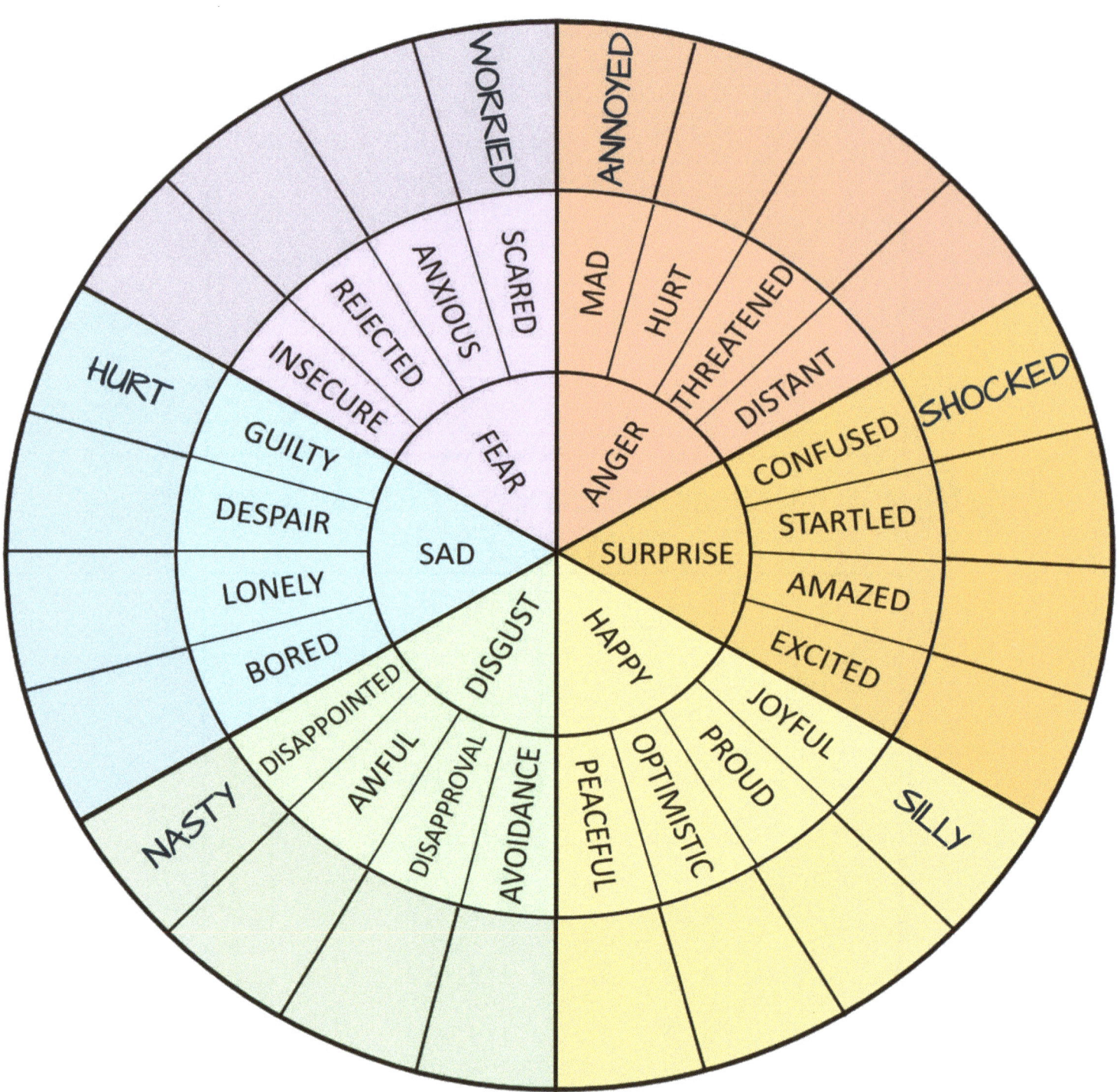

TIP!
You can make a copy of this to put with your journal or hang on your wall!

Changing Your Thoughts Worksheet

What happened?

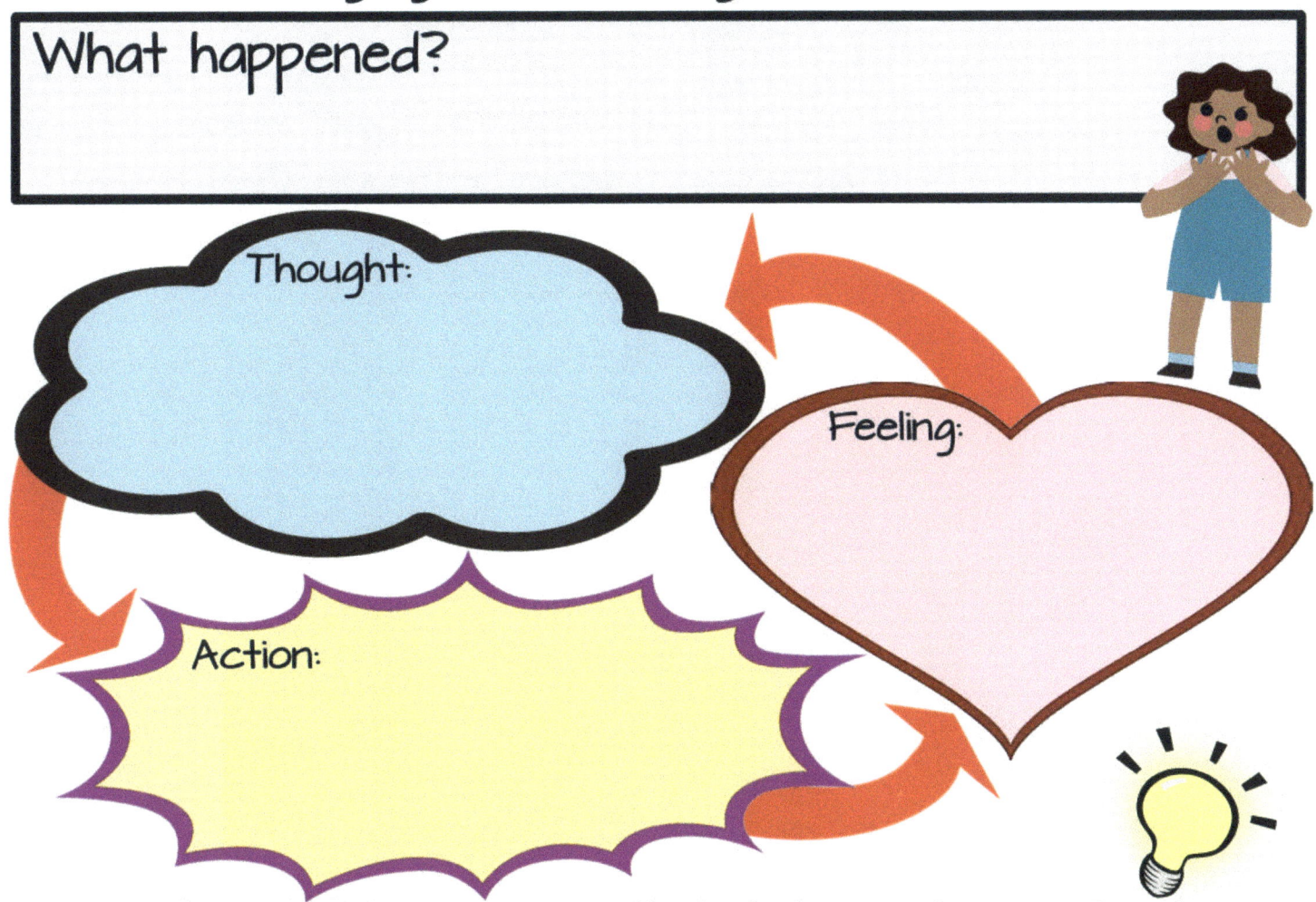

- Thought:
- Feeling:
- Action:

Remember, just because you think it does not mean it is true. Try to come up with new thoughts to see what might change.

	New Thoughts	New Feelings	New Actions
#1			
#2			
#3			

Deep Breathing Tips!

Try Flower and Candle!

Smell the flower, take a big breath in through your nose. Then blow out the candle with a big breath out through your mouth. Do it again and again until you feel better.

You can also try box breathing!
Trace the arrows with your finger and follow the steps. Breathe in and count to 4, hold your breath and count to 4, breathe out and count to 4, hold your breath and count to 4. Follow the box around until you feel better.

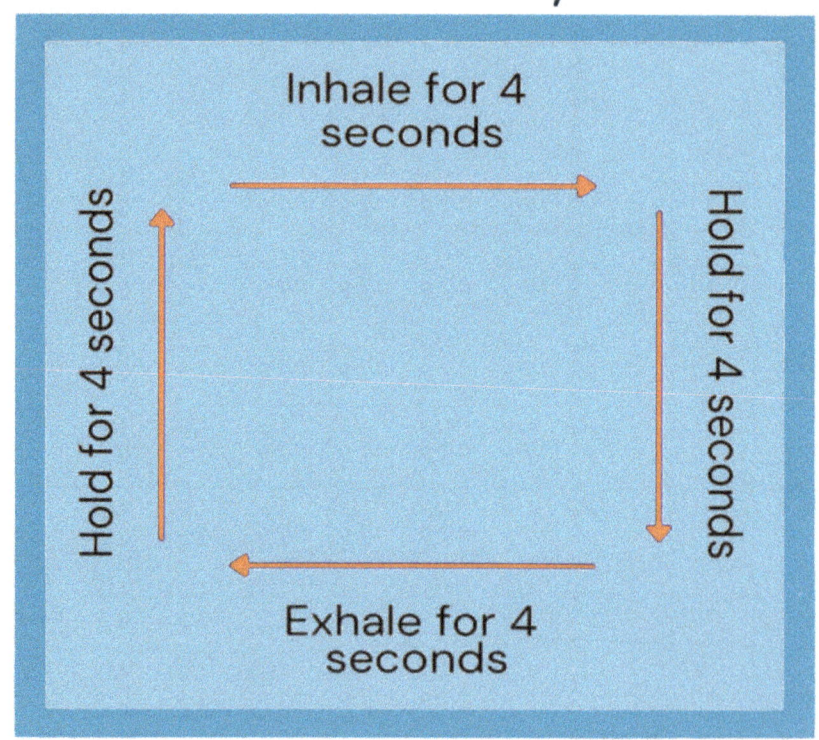

Journal Prompt

Today's date is: _____

The weather today was _____

One thing I did today was _____
_____
_____
_____

A big emotion I felt today was _____

I used these coping skills today: _____
_____
_____

Using coping skills made me feel _____
_____
_____

I am grateful for _____
_____

Tomorrow, I would like to _____
_____

Coping A to Z

Fill in the chart with a **coping** skill that starts with each letter of the alphabet. For example: (S) sleep or (Q) quiet.

A _____ B _____ C _____

D _____ E _____ F _____

G _____ H _____ I _____

J _____ K _____ L _____

M _____ N _____ O _____

P _____ Q _____ R _____

S _____ T _____ U _____

V _____ W _____ X _____

Y _____ Z _____

What is your favorite **coping** skill? _____

TIP!
Make a copy of this to hang on your wall or keep in your desk!

What am I feeling? How can I cope?

Instructions:
1. Think about how you feel.
2. Write down or circle your feelings.
3. Use your coping skills to help you feel better.

How do you feel right now?

Physical Feelings:
- Relaxed
- Sweaty
- Weak
- Fast Heartbeat
- Slow Heartbeat
- Head Hurts
- Upset Stomach
- Sleepy
- Cold
- Hot
- Other: _____

Emotional Feelings:
- Angry
- Excited
- Disgusted
- Happy
- Surprised
- Fearful
- Frustrated
- Loved
- Calm
- Sad
- Other: _____

Circle your **primary emotions** (what you feel first):

Happy   Surprise   Sad   Disgust   Fear   Anger   Other:_____

Circle your **secondary emotions** (what comes after):

Joyful   Proud   Peaceful   Excited   Amazed   Confused
Startled   Mad   Hurt   Threated   Distant   Scared   Guilty
Anxious   Rejected   Lonely   Bored   Avoidant   Other:_____

What emotion do you want to feel? _____

What **coping** skill can you use to feel better?

_____
_____

Draw how you feel on the person.
Draw what your face looks like.
Draw arrows pointing to physical feelings you feel in your body.

What primary emotion do you feel? _____

Which secondary emotions do you feel?
_____
_____

What coping skills can you use?
_____
_____

Are you feeling bad about how you behaved or reacted?
Let's review so we do not do it again!
Pretend YOU have a time machine!
You are going to go back in time
and change your reaction!
What happened?

_____

_____

What primary emotion did you feel?

_____

What secondary emotions did you feel?

_____

What physical feelings did you feel?

_____

What bad or negative thought did you have?

_____

After using the time machine, what good thought do you have?

_____

How does this make you feel now?
What primary and secondary emotions do you feel?

_____

Instead of reacting in a way that made you feel bad,
how do you act or behave after reframing your thoughts?

_____

Name one other way you can cope if this happens again:

_____

www.ingramcontent.com/pod-product-compliance
Lightning Source LLC
Chambersburg PA
CBHW042358030426
42337CB00032B/5151